THE CURRICULUM: CHRISTIAN PERSPECTIVES

ALAN BROWN

The National Society (Church of England)
for Promoting Religious Education

The National Society
Church House
Great Smith Street
London SW1P 3NZ

ISBN 0 901819 52 2

Published 1997 by The National Society (Church of England) for Promoting Religious Education

© *The National Society (Church of England) for Promoting Religious Education 1997*

All rights reserved. No part of this publication may be reproduced or stored or transmitted by any means or in any form, electronic or mechanical, including photocopying, recording, or any information storage and retrieval system without written permission which should be sought from the Copyright Manager, The National Society, Church House, Great Smith Street, London SW1P 3NZ.

'Education' (p.20) from Giles and Melville Harcourt, *Short Prayers for Long Days* is reproduced by permission of HarperCollins*Publishers* Limited.

Printed in England by Bourne Press Ltd

Contents

			Page
Foreword			v
Introduction			1
1	Educational issues		5
2	Common educational values		8
3	Differing approaches to the curriculum		15
	(i)	The curriculum in a voluntary aided primary school *Tricia Kirkham*	15
	(ii)	A Christian approach to the curriculum *Ruth Deakin Crick*	20
	(iii)	Religious Education and history: A view from the city *Roy Hughes*	24
	(iv)	The curriculum in Church of England Secondary schools *Peter Shepherd*	26
4	Christian beliefs		36
5	The values in education and the community		38
6	Spiritual development: An approach for all schools *Robin Protheroe*		43
Conclusion			46
Contributors			48

Foreword

When Robert Waddington, then Secretary of The National Society and General Synod Board of Education, wrote *A Future in Partnership* (National Society, 1984) it seemed the 1980s might be the decade of partnership. Even if that were the case, and it is open to debate, the 1990s has been the decade of choice and diversity, at least to date. The consequences of the Education Reform Act (1988) have come alive in the subsequent years and, at the time of writing, there is another Bill en route through Parliament which aims to increase selection.

The Churches, particularly the Anglican and Roman Catholic Churches, have been caught up in this tidal wave of change. This is not to demean the activities of the Free Churches, who have also been directly involved in the forefront of educational change and development; but Anglicans and Roman Catholics, with nearly 7000 schools between them, share in dealing directly with the central issues of administration and management.

This booklet is intended to raise some of the concerns of Christians regarding the curriculum. It replaces the first booklet The National Society published in its series *The Curriculum* (National Society, 1990). Perhaps because it was the first, it lacked some of the bite, even controversy, that has surrounded its successors, although it would be impossible to draw together in one short booklet all the implications of curricular changes over the last six to eight years. The intention of The National Society's series of booklets is to provoke, but provoke thoughtfully.

On this occasion, therefore, the booklet reflects upon some of the developments since 1990 – six long years labouring in the vineyard – with a particular emphasis on values and spiritual development in the curriculum. The work of some people at the sharp end of those changes, namely headteachers, has been used to demonstrate how they have had to re-define their thinking.

Have we now, in 1997, finally arrived at the plateau of stability? It would be good to think so, but a General Election, the revision of

Foreword

A/AS levels, the huge increase of students in Higher Education, the changes in Further Education, together with the advent of nursery vouchers, current interest in moral values in schools and the inspection of spiritual, moral, social and cultural development to a more critical extent, seem to suggest a vertical cliff-face rather than a plateau.

I would like to thank the many readers who made helpful (and otherwise!) critical suggestions. The responsibility for the contents and the order of the contributions is mine alone.

Alan Brown

Introduction

The Christian assumptions of many people in Britain, whether cloaked in humanist guise or not, mean that while a number of people may not attend a church regularly they continue to look to the Church(es) to ensure that moral and spiritual guidance is available, promoted and advocated. In an educational context this can mean that religion and morals become a 'slot' in the life of a school, conveniently divorcing it from the rest of the curriculum. Even Department for Education and Employment terminology uses the word 'secular' to describe that part of the curriculum which excludes RE and School Collective Worship; in other words, at least 95 per cent of the curriculum is 'secular'. This has been justified by legislators at the Department because it was used in the Education Act (1944), Section 23, and in subsequent statutory instruments, e.g. the number of hours of secular instruction to be given each day.

This is not enough for those Christians who wish to present their faith as being concerned with the whole of life and thereby necessarily influencing the whole curriculum in schools; for such Christians feel able to make a positive contribution to those areas of development which were laid down in the Education Reform Act (1988), Section 1 (2a):

(2) The curriculum for a maintained school satisfies the requirements of this section if it is a balanced and broadly based curriculum which:

   (a) promotes the spiritual, moral, cultural, mental and physical development of pupils at the school and of society,

   (b) prepares such pupils for the opportunities, responsibilities and experiences of adult life.

(This is now Section 351 of the Education Act (1996).)

The foundations a school provides should not separate learning the experiences of life and the development of spiritual and moral values from an understanding of one's place in society.

We will need to return to the development of spiritual and moral values in a separate section because of the concern of the School Curriculum and Assessment Authority (SCAA) for values in education and society. In theory, SCAA's concern is for spiritual and moral values but as spiritual values are so much more nebulous and far more difficult to define, by default it has been easier to concentrate on morality. In fact, as we shall see, it is not always possible for Christians, and perhaps other religious people too, to make simplistic divisions between spiritual and moral dimensions of life. But more of that later.

The 1990s witnessed the implementation of the National Curriculum; it also demonstrated the dangers of legislating in haste. In the House of Lords, during the progress of the Education Reform Bill in 1987/88, Lord Joseph, a former Secretary of State for Education, had warned against placing too great a weight upon the National Curriculum. His words bore fruit in the 1990s when Sir Ron Dearing at the National Curriculum Council and then at SCAA slimmed down the much vaunted curriculum so that it could actually be taught in the time available. Teachers had worked hard to create schemes of work matching the legal requirements of the National Curriculum but soon discovered these would have to be rewritten to meet the requirements of the National Curriculum Mark 2. It was a time of morale-sapping despair for many teachers, not least because it coincided with the creation of the Office for Standards in Education (OFSTED). (Wales has its own inspection arrangements and its own curriculum authority. As this booklet is concerned with general principles relevant to all schools in England and Wales, it has not documented the Welsh inspection and curriculum agencies in every case.) Many teachers, particularly in primary schools, felt, perhaps incorrectly, that they were to be inspected on aspects of the curriculum that had not been fully developed and for which they had not been properly trained.

There does need to be a willingness to give thanks, however, for the recognition that teachers were overburdened and schools hamstrung by the enormity of the change. In 1990, *The Curriculum* (National Society, 1990) pointed out:

> Documents, however experimental, provisional or exploratory, have a habit of becoming tablets of stone, with consequent problems. Christians need no reminding of how a rigid response to the letter of the text can be inhibiting.

That comment was timely. Of course there are still problems with the National Curriculum, but changes have been made; there is now a more realistic demand made of teachers and clearer, more directive, support is available to them through the National Curriculum Orders and the framework provided for inspection by OFSTED. The new inspection system is bedding down and while still being diagnostic rather than advisory, it is generally being regarded with less fear and beginning to be recognised as having a more positive, constructive face.

For the Anglican Church the place of denominational schools has continued to be a matter of major interest. For some voluntary controlled schools it came as a shock that they were to be inspected under Section 13 of the 1992 Schools Inspection Act (now Section 23 of the Schools Inspection Act (1996)).

The 'church relatedness' of some voluntary schools had been lost in the seeds of time: the startling realisation that worship had to be in line with the Trust Deed, and that the Church should and would be interested in how such schools related to the local church community, caused more than a flutter in some dovecotes.

There was, and continues to be, a growing concern about secularism across the whole curriculum and an insidious trend to compartmentalise spiritual and moral development into Religious Education. The other side of this coin was the restlessness of some religious groups with a perceived growing secularism or with church schools that did not appear to meet the needs of their multi-faith communities. Is it not remarkable that *The Durham Report*, published by The National Society and the Society for Promoting Christian Knowledge as recently as 1970, could overlook the multi-faith nature of so many Church schools?

RE, RI or RS?

It may be that a curious mis-application of terminology has confused the issue for Church schools in particular. When, in the 1988 Education Reform Act, RI (Religious Instruction), the term used in the 1944 Education Act, was changed to RE (Religious Education), it was welcomed as a step forward. The use of 'RI' was recognised, by implication, as having no educational rationale. There is an area of dysfunction, however, in relation to Church schools. If one refers to the Religious Education received by the pupil in a Church school, is one referring to the curriculum subject or the whole religious experience of the pupil at that school, all of which contributes to her/his religious education? In a Church school, in any city or village, made up of Church-going Anglicans or children from the local Muslim community, would not the broad use of 'Religious Education' be a more appropriate term for the whole experience of the pupil in the school? If that were the case, would pupils acquire a better understanding of the role of religion in life?

Should the academic study of religion be 'Religious Studies', freeing Religious Education to meet this broad religious experience?

It may be that out of a growing concern over secularism, with the increasing multi-faith nature of society, and a belief that Religious Experience (RE) was more important than Religious Information (RI), that the Christian schools movement gathered momentum. Why should Christian parents not have their children educated in an environment within which the Christian integrity of every curriculum subject could be explored? And if this were to be true for Christians, why not for Muslims, Jews, Hindus, etc.?

One area where the faith communities were expected to make a distinctive contribution was in the religious and spiritual development of pupils across the whole curriculum. It is, therefore, surprising that only in 1996 did SCAA draw together a Forum which provided a platform on which such contribution could be made. The Churches in particular wished to underscore the importance of the spiritual dimension in every aspect of the curriculum and the whole life of the school. But could this be defined in such a way that (a) it could gain general approval and (b) it could be measured and inspected?

1

Educational issues

Values

It appears easier to locate responsibility for the development of values in some areas of the curriculum than in others: indeed it may be that in the content of the curriculum, values are more pertinent in some places than in others. It is, however, a denial of professional integrity for a teacher to assume that some areas of the curriculum can be excused responsibility for the formation and promotion of values. The curriculum is not content alone: the pedagogy of teaching, its methods and strategies, the relationships between school and pupil, teacher and pupil, all contribute to the total development of the values promoted and suported within a school.

The National Society has sought to contribute to this area in its range of booklets, particularly those on *Spiritual Development* (1996) and *Moral Education* (1995). It will publish two further booklets on *Social Development* and *Cultural Development* in 1997.

Competition and co-operation

It would be difficult to deny that competition can be positive; what cause concern are the attitudes and values that often accompany competition. Competition is too often represented as a negative feature of education; this is unfortunate, for in much competition there has to be co-operation e.g. most team games, groupwork on projects, form or year activities. The ability to learn to work with others, though not necessarily in a competitive situation, must be one of the more important characteristics of the mature adult. Competitiveness has to be complemented with the recognition that all pupils, all people, have a special value in themselves. It is unfortunate if competition and co-operation are regarded as opposites.

They may be in conflict, but they offer a healthy tension which should not be ignored. Competition can draw out greater and finer achievements and should not always be artificially discouraged; indeed on occasions it should be encouraged.

Support, comfort and honour should form an essential response to apparent (or self-assessed) failure. One of the Christian principles of education has been, and must continue to be, the support of those who believe they have failed. We all have to learn how to manage and cope with failure. One way in which we retain our integrity and self-respect as human beings is by sharing our failure with others and with God. Learning to live with failure is a part of maturing; to hold failure within its own context and to recognise that in failure lies the seed of self-awareness and self-understanding is to discover that in death there is life. It is by recognising failure and dealing with it positively that we are re-born. The agony caused by the pressure of possible failure is something which Christians share with the deep humanity Jesus revealed at stressful times in his life, not least prior to the Crucifixion.

Individual and community

Schools as institutions have a corporate quality. Indeed each community, being more than a collection of individuals, is necessarily corporate, and our responses as Christians should be to the needs of each individual so that we may affect the whole. The curriculum alone cannot establish the true ethos of a school, nor can the ethos be accidental, for it is created by the love, care and professional concern with which staff, pupils and the community interrelate. It would be difficult to affirm the Christian ethos of Church schools if the manifestation of the Christian faith were not apparent in personal relationships, in admissions policies, in the relationship with local Christian communities; if it were not present in symbol, name and focus. In the County school, also, there are teachers who wish to contribute to the ethos of their school by being true to the depth of their Christian faith. The ethos of a school cannot be an afterthought: it is a collection of positive values – including honesty, love, integrity, commitment, forgiveness, co-operation – to which the Christian often makes a major contribution. One-sided individualism is not Christian: neither is a one-sided emphasis on community. The symbol of the two arms of the Cross with truth at the centre is as relevant here as elsewhere.

The inspection of schools and the attendant concern and publicity about values, school ethos, spiritual and moral education, etc. has highlighted this area of education. Both OFSTED and SCAA (and indeed the old National Curriculum Council) have all wrestled with these difficult aspects of education. The current fashion in education for measuring achievement and attainment may be a hindrance, as many contributory factors are often in the very areas which fight shy of assessment. And yet, if these aspects of a school are to be inspected, should one not be able to measure success? The April 1996 OFSTED inspection criteria are more sympathetic than the earlier attempts to define the indefinable.

Writing a paper (as yet unpublished) for the SCAA Forum on Values in Education and Community in January 1996, Professor John Hull of the University of Birmingham perhaps offered a key to resolve this tension:

'Spiritual education inspires young people to live for others. Spirituality exists not inside people but between them... spirituality is to do with solidarity and communion.'

So the space between people may be sacred; it could be spiritual. It is the tension *between* the individual and the community that is the breath of life. Schools may find it helpful to regard one aspect of their provision for spiritual development as being rooted in their sense of community and solidarity.

2
Common educational values

Some values in education are of critical importance to all teachers. It is not the intention of this chapter to claim that the professional concern teachers demonstrate is the sole property of the Christian teacher or the Church school. It is clear, however, that as Christians involved in education they will find, within themselves and in the life of the school, a particular contribution to make through which their Christian and professional commitment may be focused and expressed. Some of those common values are considered here.

Integrity and commitment

Integrity and commitment should not be confused with indoctrination. Neither Christians nor members of any other faiths or life stances should expect to use the captive audience of the classroom to promulgate their views to the exclusion or misrepresentation of all others. In a very real sense that is a denial of the concern for the development, independence and integrity of the pupil which Christians seek to nurture. A teacher's own faith is expressed through his/her professional concern for the pupils and the school community. As teacher and learner one must be honest with oneself and with others, even if this may lead to disagreement. 'Critical openness' is welcomed by some Christians as a means by which the integrity of the Gospel may be presented to pupils while continuing to have a critical appreciation of what is being studied. Not all Christians are comfortable with this: some prefer the term 'critical affirmation'.

Christians respond to the diverse needs of the pupils and of society (if indeed we recognise there is such a thing) in different ways; they have to measure educational establishments and requirements against the criteria of their own faith and commitment. There will be a variety of answers; some will differ significantly from others and the Christian's ability to cope with difference is important. At the very centre of this difference should be Christian love and the continuing search to be worthy of the Lord we choose to serve.

The pertinent question for Christians is: 'How can we hand on our Christian inheritance in such a way as to enable pupils to make a free and informed commitment or freely to withhold that commitment?' Christian education has historically been regarded as the purveyor of traditional values; it continues to extend that inheritance while acknowledging the continuing challenges of contemporary society. How do Christians respond to the challenge of a post-literate, post-modern world? Is there a breakdown of traditional authority models in society and the church? If so, how can Christians meet the consequences of developing situations?

Relationships

Schools are where human beings, Christians and others, live and work, and as such they will create their own sets of values. Christians will want to contribute to these values and ethos. The values will be reflected in the moral dilemmas discussed in the classroom and staffroom as well as in the openness and honesty of relationships. If there is a failure in relationships then the well-intended opening section of the Education Reform Act (quoted on p. 1) will be totally irrelevant.

One of the developments in schools since the Education Reform Act was implemented has been the increased importance of all policies including Equal Opportunities, Race Relations, Bullying, Sex Education. At the heart of all these has been a desire for good relationships within the school, which may flow out into the local community.

Control and discipline

The 'critical openness' referred to earlier has become a way of describing a Christian approach to oneself and to the scriptures (see also Peter Shepherd's article on p. 28). Christians should be critical of themselves while wishing to affirm the value of criticism as a means of helping them recognise and appreciate diversity within the world. Schools need to develop discipline not for the school's own sake, not as a means to an end but rather as a means of producing self-discipline in pupils to maintain that 'openness' which requires the teacher, or the school, to respond to and respect the pupil. We need to recognise that, being human, we may be self-disciplined in some aspects of life and less so in others. Self-discipline is not simply an indication of behaviour; rather, it should enable the person to develop into an effective and contributory member of society.

Discipline is not conformity or unthinking obedience; it too has a moral and value base. Legitimate challenge to existing norms and values is well documented in the Christian tradition from the confrontation between Peter and Paul up to the present day, and Christians in particular should take care when criticising others or requiring rigid acceptance of agreed norms. Those who call for discipline often mean control or 'doing what you're told'. That sort of discipline may be appropriate for word processors, computers, subordinate soldiers or children in danger but it needs normally to be set in the broader context of the network of relationships in a school committed to the development and education of the young. Christians, being alert to the whole of God's creation, to life in all its aspects, will be aware that criticism alone may be destructive and lead to decay; enthusiasm for criticism always needs to be tempered with the knowledge that it can be very threatening and/or destructive. The message from the Gospels is positive – it is a re-enforcement of what is positive: 'go and sin no more' is not a denial or dismissal of past errors, but it looks forward to what is possible and what can be.

Choice of content

In choosing what is appropriate content we reveal and express a set of values. It would be unfortunate if schools followed the requirements of the National Curriculum in a way that allowed the content of that curriculum to support, or even create, a set of values with which Christians could not be in sympathy. There have been discussions over the implications of the Science curriculum, in particular the teaching of Sex Education, as well as the exclusivity of some scientific notions of creation. Some parents may object to the selection of certain books for examination in English or to a particular interpretation of History or Geography. These are subtle and complex issues. The choice of content is an important aspect of the subject curriculum, for it sets the agenda for the development and public revelation of the values upon which the school will run.

The wholeness of the curriculum

So often in our schools the teacher in the classroom, or the head of department, still takes an enormous amount of responsibility for *what* is taught to the pupils and *how* it is taught. Is the answer in greater regimentation? Should teachers be recognised as technicians only and the options available to them be reduced? As Christians we have to struggle with the way in which our whole life offers an opportunity for our Christian commitment. At times we recognise failure and feel the thinness of faith (some will welcome the Anglican tradition of confession and reconciliation found in its formal services). We seek to maintain a balance between the wholeness and firmness of our faith faced with the individual situations which are to confirm or threaten it. This striving is to be encouraged in the curriculum of the school. A school is not a timetable of periods, a series of days, a collection of separate individuals; it is a wholeness of itself and as such the curriculum has to be finally set in the framework of school life. Teachers share their intentions, their strategies, their planning and their content with each other in order to create a coherence and wholeness in the educational experience of their pupils. We return again to critical openness, to integrity and the recognition that to be a whole person is not an accident or a series of incidents but a coherent, purposeful gathering together of the whole. If every school had an ethos which supported personal wholeness by acknowledging values of various kinds, then the coherence and wholeness of the curriculum for the pupil would become much clearer.

Developing all pupils to their potential

Many of these concerns can be gathered together in order to affirm the commitment of all teachers, Christians and others, to their pupils. About 20 per cent of pupils have special educational needs of one sort or another at some point in their schooldays. Of course, professional teachers will have a commitment to this large but constantly changing group, but for Christians these pupils represent a particular concern. While all pupils should be encouraged to develop to the fullest degree, some, including the specially gifted, may need more help and support than others. The historical and theological concern that Christians have had for the poor and the underprivileged should ensure that such pupils will be fully provided for in all aspects of school life. The image of God, *Imago Dei*, is in the forefront of a Christian vision of human potential. God became a human being so human beings could be one in God; this, for Christians, is life lived in its fullness.

Links in the chain

In each of the above sections there is a clear Christian insight derived from the Bible, the church and the theological rationale that underpins Christians in education. Each section could stand alone in the sense that the values espoused *could* be shared by a secular humanist or a member of another faith community. For Christians, however, any involvement with education needs to be rooted in Tradition, Scripture and Reason – for unless there is a vision of discipleship scored deeply into educational thinking, there are but shallow roots.

As Christians, we need to be sure that we do not withhold God, and the beliefs, values and practices associated with God, from children. The distinction between nurture and education has become, correctly, blurred; all education is a form of nurture. There can be no reason to withhold exploration about God and about theology from pupils. If mindless indoctrination is to be avoided, then so are the forms of militant evangelistic secularism which may be found in some classrooms. Indoctrination is not confined to religions.

The irony of Christianity is that the cross opens wide its arms presenting itself to the world: vulnerable yet powerful; naked yet confident. This comes alive for Christian educators not in a pious simplistic manner but in the values and beliefs held up for examination by pupils (and staff) in the context of a life's journey, where the soft-focus montage of spiritual sentimentality is more than matched by the serrated edges of real life. The Christian belief in the Incarnation secures the vulnerability of God (i.e. a paradox in itself) in human history and in the life of a person. For this reason, if for no other, Docetism (the belief that Jesus was not fully human but only 'appeared' to be so) had to fail, for it was the will of God to be emptied into a human person that provided the means by which Christians could move towards a deeper understanding of the very nature of God.

What can Christians in every school do, whether they are staff, parents, governors or, of course, pupils?

They can ask questions about:

(a) the quality, provision and planning of worship;

(b) the quality, provision and planning of religious education;

(c) how the spiritual and moral development policies impinge upon the aims of every aspect of school life;

(d) whether there is an allocation in the budget for staff to be trained to support worship, RE, spiritual and moral development;

(e) whether there is support from the churches for schools (see D. Lankshear, *Churches Serving Schools*, National Society, 1996);

(f) whether the school is concerned about integrity, relationships, discipline and self-discipline;

(g) if the school can produce a rationale for the whole curriculum which helps all pupils develop to their full potential.

3

Differing approaches to the curriculum

In this section of the booklet four of the five contributors look at the curriculum from different but related points of view. Tricia Kirkham weighs up the demands of Church schools against the needs of the whole curriculum, while Ruth Deakin Crick demonstrates that the theology and practice underpinning an independent Christian school would not be very different from the theology of many state-maintained Church schools. Roy Hughes considers the very specific contribution that RE in the context of the Humanities can make to values and attitudes; and Peter Shepherd takes the view that Christian Education is the means to an end, and therefore the Church school curriculum should reflect that fundamental premise.

(i) The curriculum in a voluntary aided primary school

Tricia Kirkham

What makes a Voluntary Aided school different from a County school – apart from the letters after its name?

This question can be very difficult for staff and Governors to answer. Inevitably, we think of the aims of the school, of the ethos and atmosphere and of the spiritual and moral dimension. But what about the curriculum? Does being a Voluntary Aided school make any difference to that? If you believe that the aims of the school are driving, and reflected in, every aspect of the school, then certainly Voluntary Aided status should be visible in the curriculum. Deciding where and what part it should play is less obvious, however.

Spirituality

Starting with the spiritual element, it is easy to see where this fits into the daily act of worship and RE, but it should percolate through all areas of the curriculum and affect every part of school life, reflecting the creative process of God acting through us as humans. For children this can mean having their attention drawn to aspects such as the mystery of growth and new life in Science; or the wonder of the human body in Movement; in Art and English, the beauty and power of words and images, or the mystery of infinity or shape and order in Mathematics.

Giving the children such opportunities is, while very valuable, not enough. It is part of the role of the Voluntary Aided school to draw these reflections back to God, and to anchor them in an awareness of God at work both in the world around us and in and through each one of us. Awe and wonder can give the Church school the chance to show children God's presence behind and within those 'special' moments of beauty, mystery, stillness and peace. If as Christians we believe everything comes from God and is given to us by him, we need to pause sometimes to think how wonderful and amazing that really is. Therefore, we have a further duty to use and care for those gifts for the benefit of others *and* to the glory of God.

Now this may sound, however worthy, very heavy stuff for a primary school, and perhaps something that presents difficulties for teachers lacking personal belief or sensitivity. This is where there is a need for whole-school policies, which are understood and achievable by all staff and within which are embedded the spiritual aims of the school; furthermore, both aims and policies need to be actively supported and upheld by Governors and the management team, so that even the most unconfident member of staff can be shown ways in which spirituality can be promoted and allowed to develop.

We can convey this to children with a lightness of touch: for example, by stopping for a moment in a maths lesson on shape to consider the beauty and complexity of pattern in God's created world and to wonder at it. It need not take a long time, it certainly doesn't need to happen *every* time, but it can serve to open the children's eyes to another dimension, or just plant the seed of a thought that there may be the opportunity to reflect on one of these issues.

There may be other times when an opportunity occurs more spontaneously, when children are suddenly struck by the power of a story or poem, by the emotion conveyed in a piece of music, or the excitement of discovery or achievement. When it suddenly began to snow, a class of Reception and Year One children rushed outside to stand looking up into the sky at the falling snow, and to taste and feel the snowflakes as they fell; when they came indoors, they were able to think how wonderful God's world is, of the vastness of the sky, the magic of snow and how lucky they were to have a warm school when they returned!

God-given gifts

As well as contemplating the wonders of God's world, there are also his gifts to us, in terms of our skills and abilities, and the responsibilities these gifts bring with them. How can we use them for good, for God? How can we develop and realise them in ourselves and others? How can we celebrate and praise achievement, and how and when do we involve God in that celebration and thanksgiving? Much of this is achieved daily in classrooms everywhere, as part of good primary practice; teachers are very good at recognising and celebrating what children do and have a myriad of ingenious ways of showing this. But for the Voluntary Aided school, the key point is the involvement of God in this valuable process; remembering that the gifts are given to us by God, that he works through us, that we need to say thank-you to him too – rather like remembering to touch base.

Perhaps in considering a design or piece of technology, we can think of the many skills God has given us that enable us to create both simple and complex pieces of engineering. For young children this may be enough in itself, but with older children it could be taken further, looking at positive and destructive ways humanity uses these God-given gifts, and wondering what God would want us to do.

On the most simplistic level, perhaps the difference between a Church school and a County school is marvelling at *God's* world and the *God-given* gifts that mean we can have warm houses and schools, and just marvelling at the world. Very often, those special and electric moments can be followed by a time in which children can bring their own thoughts and thanks to God, through prayer and reflection, either privately or together.

In the celebration of good work, or effort or achievement, we can ask the question, 'How have we been able to do this?', to draw attention to the gifts God has given to us, and how we are able to use them.

God in action

In sharing and enjoying these moments with the children, we can also use them as examples of God in action. We can help children understand that God is not some ancient, far-removed figure, but present and active around us all the time. We are part of his created world, and as such, he also works *through* us (remember the prayer of St Teresa of Avila, which is often used at Ascension: 'Christ has no body now on earth but yours, no hands but yours, no feet but yours; yours are the eyes through which to look at Christ's compassion to the world, yours are the feet with which he is to go about doing good, and yours are the hands with which he is to bless us now.').

Policies and practicalities

We must ensure that we do this in a systematic rather than serendipitous way, however. These elements need to be built into our policies – as key elements in the policy statements – and then interpreted into action points in the units and schemes of work. We can then make sure that we fulfil and deliver this very important role and responsibility. We also need to ensure that staff have the help and support they need to uphold the aims and deliver the policies.

The ethos of the school is vitally important in setting the tone. It is much easier to say 'Come and see, or rather, feel', than to attempt to describe something so nebulous. However, there are discernible factors that contribute very positively to a school's ethos. The physical environment is one: the way in which a school is cared for, the standard and quality as well as the content, subject and purpose of displays, signs and symbols of belief and Christian commitment, will show whether God is at the centre of the school and a part of every classroom. Worship is another, and in a Voluntary Aided school, this should be an act of *worship* with a strongly and clearly defined spiritual element, rather than just a moral tale or a chance to give out school notices. Another element is the attitude of children and adults to one another and to visitors. This may be encapsulated in the behaviour policy, for example, or the marking policy, or the role the school plays within the local and wider community.

Working as a whole school to create and put into action policies is vital. Governors, staff, parents and pupils can all contribute to the policy-making process and in doing so will know, own and understand those policies. From the broad base will come its strength, and through this, support can be given to staff and pupils alike. Many teachers, and indeed some staff in Voluntary Aided schools are not committed Christians, and will therefore rely on the guidance given in policies and schemes of work. By weaving the Christian aims of the school, the spirituality, the elements that create the ethos, the awareness of God, his work, world and gifts to us, into *all* areas of the curriculum and into every policy statement, Governors, Heads and Management Teams in schools can ensure that the aims are indeed upheld in a carefully regulated, measured and developmental way and are at the heart of the school. Perhaps the responsibility of the Voluntary Aided school is to be overt in its Christian affirmation, so that *all* the curriculum (including spiritual, moral and social) flows out of an acknowledgement of God's presence and God's love, and this will be seen, not just in the outcomes in terms of children's learning, but in the creation of policies, the expectations (of all employed in the school and children), the appointment of staff, in fact in every aspect of school life.

> *Education*
>
> We teach religion all day long
>
> We teach it in arithmetic, by accuracy.
>
> We teach it in language, by learning to say what we mean - yea, yea, or nay, nay.
>
> We teach it in history, by humanity.
>
> We teach it in geography, by breadth of mind.
>
> We teach it in handicraft, by thoroughness
>
> We teach it in astronomy, by reverence.
>
> We teach it by good manners to one another, and by truthfulness in all things. We teach students to build the Church of Christ out of the actual relationships in which they stand to their teachers and to their school fellows.
>
> Giles and Melville Harcourt, *Short Prayers for Long Days*

(ii) A Christian approach to the curriculum
Ruth Deakin Crick

There is no such thing as a value-free curriculum. All programmes of learning, including the National Curriculum, are shaped by the ideas and values of those who design them. The knowledge and skills which are selected (or not selected) for attention, the teaching and learning styles adopted in delivery, the mode of organisation of the curriculum and the ethos of the classroom are all powerfully influenced by ideas, values and beliefs about children, society and knowledge. The question then for Christian schools is, how should the ideas, beliefs and values which constitute the foundation of the school shape the actual praxis of teaching and learning in the school?

In days of self-management, diversity and choice within a quasi-market system of provision, these questions are very important. Equally significant are the deeper cultural changes which our society is experiencing – described by some as post-modernity. This is characterised by global economies, the loss of faith in a universalising belief system, lifestyle politics, self-actualisation, the compression of time and space, the information explosion, and not least the sense of moral confusion. These influences in our culture can also profoundly influence education and present Christian schools with new opportunities to be distinctive. I will seek to outline a way of understanding and delivering a distinctively Christian curriculum.

The starting-point for a Christian curriculum is the experience of God, through the love of Christ, which leads to an understanding of the world, of humanity and a hope for the future that is summarised in the great creeds or statements of faith. However, it is impossible to get straight from a statement of faith to educational practice without going through an important phase of interpretation. Here, an essential component of the process, are teachers who are reflectively committed to examining their practice in the light of educational theory and the ideas, beliefs and values which constitute the Christian faith. These teachers also need to be able to critique their own culture, and to understand the world-view commitments behind the National Curriculum.

Another phase in the process is the articulation of a world- and life-view that is consistent with the Christian faith. That is a world-view which assumes that there is a created natural world existing independently of our knowing of it, and which we explore through the natural sciences, and develop through technology. However, we are human beings who understand ourselves and our world in story form and knowing can never be value-free. The exploration of the social world through the humanities and arts is always seen through the lens of the thought-forms of our own culture. While there may be much in our own culture that has already been influenced by the Judaeo-Christian traditions, as Christians we need to understand how the Christian story interacts with the story of our own and other cultures. In some ways the heart of Christian education is to help learners to understand how three stories relate to each other – the learner's own story; the stories of their own and other cultures; and the story of God's involvement in human history.

To do this we need to equip our students with an ability to think critically, and personally to engage with their own learning. One useful model to achieve this is for schools to identify a set of values which are derived from the Christian faith and to incorporate those within their own educational vision statement and aims. For example, one of the great Christian values is the loving stewardship of natural resources. This can be derived directly from the cultural mandate in Genesis and is of direct relevance to us today. This value can form part of a framework of values, which teachers and pupils consciously seek to work with, in practice and in theory. Studies in science, history, geography and many other disciplines can incorporate a critique from the perspective of stewardship. This is a useful means of integrating spiritual and moral development across the curriculum. The value framework of the school is important in providing a tool for critique, since criticism always proceeds from a particular framework or world-view. The value framework can also be seen as a set of norms or principles by which those in the school community seek to live.

While many of the values which a Christian school would endorse would also be accepted in secular schools, for example loving our neighbours as ourselves, or justice, or excellence, a Christian school is able to root these values into a living tradition. The school assemblies can highlight the spiritual aspects of these values: justice for Christians, for example, is found in the cross of Christ, and the Religious Education syllabus can explore them theologically from a Christian perspective as well as from the perspective of other faiths. It is important, too, that at some stage in the curriculum the secular belief systems of our culture are examined against the framework of the school's values.

Curriculum organisation and the construction and selection of syllabi is a critical task for the Christian school. A Christian approach to the teaching of science, for example, would affirm that there is a created world which we can explore and understand rationally, and which we can develop technologically. However that scientific knowing would not be the supreme form of knowledge. Science taught from a Christian world-view may well approach the subject-matter as a whole, to give students a holistic framework within which to understand the natural world and its part in God's story, rather than choosing a more fragmented and atomised approach.

Modern foreign languages similarly need to be underpinned by content and methodologies which are consistent with a Christian world-view, and would introduce foreign countries as places with histories, contemporary problems and real storied people, rather than simply as places for individual consumers to travel to. All of the disciplines in a Christian school need to be critiqued, assessed and developed by those who teach, in response to the needs and situations of particular schools, and in dialogue with the truth claims of the Christian faith. The curriculum is a dynamic process, but the content does matter, and it is not neutral.

Overall, many Christian schools seek to develop an integral approach to the curriculum, which presents a holistic view of the world to the learners. Geography is related to history and to science, and all of these subjects are important ways of understanding, critiquing and making choices in our world. Primary schools naturally integrate their subjects. At secondary level the department structures make this more difficult, but with vision and commitment it can be done. The possibilities for the integration of knowledge presented by Information Technology and Design Technology are particularly useful, and represent new and challenging fields for curriculum design which reflects a Christian world-view.

Finally, an essential component of a Christian commitment is critical openness on the part of teachers and learners. The school's task is education; the task of the Church is to do with nurture within a particular faith. Whilst a school should promote a given set of values, it is especially important that it does so with a spirit of critique! The mode of critique, including a critique of Christian belief, is very important if learners are going to make sense of their world and as Christians find ways of understanding it and living in it in the light of their own experience. It is also important for keeping the tradition of Christianity alive in our schools.

(iii) Religious Education and history: A view from the city

Roy Hughes

St Paul's Church of England Voluntary Aided Primary School (New Windsor) is an urban primary school distant from the bookladen citadels of the middle-class. The school is situated in deepest Salford; many of our children do not belong to church-going families.

Religious Education is a complex and demanding subject, not to be trifled with. It is, too, an enormous subject: its pedagogy can be perplexing. In this article I am largely concerned with part of the 'outcome' of an RE programme and with a hybrid approach.

The school has been involved, from its beginnings, with the development of the teaching of history in the primary years. The connections between history and religious education have proved a fertile ground for the development of such, but not all, of an RE programme. The earliest recognition was that history gives us *all* different and discrete religious cultures. In practical terms the School was able to draw on SCAA's Model Syllabuses (1994) where the exploration of Attainment Targets and Attitudes in Religious Education gives a firm underpinning to our approach. The understanding of structure in this SCAA publication lifts it above the run of other works on the pedagogy of Religious Education.

Also important for us have been:

- *Religious Education: a local curricular framework* (SCAA/NCC 1991). This provides a useful structure for the linkage between RE and other curricular areas, in a post-Education Reform Act format.

- *The Diocese of Manchester Syllabus for Religious Education* (1994). A comprehensive survey and a further reminder of the symbiotic relationship between the pedagogy of RE and History.

- *Religious Education in the Primary School* (National Society, 1996). A serious and informed exploration of the disparate and complex elements in the RE programme: this takes a valuable wide focus.

A programme of Religious Education can do many things. In its essence it needs to engage children in making meaning (see G. Wells, *The Meaning Makers*, Hodder & Stoughton, 1987). In this domain RE is obviously powerful for it looks to **empathy, motivation** and **identification.** History, too, is strong here – the aspiration is for the child to make sense of the world. This is the foundation of effective learning and where Religious Education has a vital place. That place is not always recognised when it has become necessary to identify the roles and relationships that good, well-resourced and well-taught Religious Education can forge.

A list of strategies, processes and concerns shared with history readily becomes apparent, and to choreograph them is not over-difficult and can be a fruitful area for developing study skills.

- **Investigation**: asking children to examine evidence and gather information.

- **Imagination**: not used here, in the sense of invention or flight of fancy, but rather to hypothesise: to use evidence in the consideration of the range of likely outcomes.

- **The acquisition of knowledge**: teachers need in RE to be conscious of the delicacy of an approach to knowledge which can challenge faith, even destroy it, as well as creating and maintaining it. Sensitivity in this area is necessary, but many young children are engrossed by information and information gathering.

- **The development of analysis**: asking children to look at evidence and to determine what might be belief, what might be fact, what might be both (or neither) and what might be the relationship between them.

The **development of values** in history and **attitudes in religious education** is a further part of that communality and intimacy they share. The development of values and attitudes is a great expectation of pupils, and should be central in the Humanities.

Among the values and attitudes I would count as most valuable:

- **Respect and tolerance**: a respect for those with different beliefs and a tolerance of value systems different to one's own.

- An **understanding** of where, and why, we are now, based on acquired knowledge and analysis.

- A **sense of diversity** because of the plurality of beliefs, customs, traditions and artefacts.

This is not intended to be a detailed exploration of the pedagogy of religious education in the context of a Church school. The use of story (again, shared with history in the primary years) would have a central place in any such discussion and I have not been able to examine that place here. Nor have I entered the world of emotional or symbolic meaning and, of course, our best efforts still leave much to be desired. If what has been described above were the whole diet of RE, it would be a simplistic and an incomplete view of a central area in the development of the child and the curriculum. What *is* clear is the important and shared place of religious education in the pedagogy of humanities in primary school education in England. This has been explored to great effect most notably in the (pioneering) work of A. Blyth *et al.* (*Curriculum Planning*, Collins-ESL, 1976), and more recently by A. Pollard and M.J. Drummond (*Humanities and Primary Education*, London, 1995) and G. Bage (*The Purposes of History in Schools*, Cambridge, 1996)), in their writings on inter-disciplinary approaches to learning in the primary years. The use of such ped-agogy, familiar to me first from history in the early years, has wound the mainspring of my approach to religious education. It is an approach that is notably 'un-illusioned', looking to common strategies, common values and real learning for the young child in religious education.

(iv) The curriculum in Church of England secondary schools
Peter Shepherd

Church schools should be distinctive. If they are not distinctive then there would seem little point in the Church being involved in the delivery of education towards the end of the twentieth century. We recognise its historic input with gratitude and praise, but why not now leave it all to the State (or to the private sector, some would wish to add)? So we claim a distinctive ethos for our Church schools. But what precisely is it? 'Ethos' is a very elusive concept; so slippery, indeed, that it often obfuscates (sometimes deliberately, we might think) more than it clarifies. Teasing out the concept would be time-consuming, but without doubt our findings would include:

- centrality of worship for the community

- quality of relationships within the school and with the community it serves and with specific regard to the curriculum

- provision of a 'Christian context' for learning

But again (we might be asked), what exactly is a Christian context for learning? Is it the provision of what is often, somewhat uncritically, called 'Christian education', or at least 'a Christian-based education'? The problem has the nature of paradox, for some would argue that Christianity itself is actually inimical to education! The case for the defence cannot simply be assumed, and certainly needs to be explored and answered before we can make progress on the more detailed issues.

It is absolutely true that 'education' derives not from the Latin root *educere* (with the potentially rich notion of 'leading out'), but from *educare*, meaning 'to train', thus connoting more than a little in the way of indoctrination (when you train someone, they do as you say). Nevertheless the former is a far more appropriate and helpful (albeit inaccurate) source of ideas from which derives our modern understanding of what it might mean 'to educate'. Such ideas are often summed up in the term 'a liberal education'. Despite a continuing debate that so often appears to set education against (vocational) training (with the tendency to try to make education simply a socio-economic tool), even the provision of a 'liberal education' should not be literally useless. Neither will it be simply utilitarian.

What it stresses will often sound like a collection of clichés: 'educating the whole person', 'education for life', 'design for living', etc. But there are supremely important values embedded here, which are all about what it means to be human. We must not forget that systems of education will themselves project clearly enough those values which are important to a particular society. The education system of Nazi Germany, for example, was based on the principles of *Herrenvolk* (master-race), *Fuhrerprinzip* (absolute obedience to the leader) and the nationalist doctrine of *Blut und Boden* (i.e. race and Fatherland). This provides an object lesson in what education is not about. Nazi education was an indoctrinating process which encouraged intolerance (of foreigners and, of course, especially Jews), blind obedience (instead of enabling children to think for themselves) and an ultimately destructive nationalism. It is of great interest that SCAA has continued to press for the teaching through History of what it would presumably call a 'positive nationalism'. While I am not suggesting that nationalism can never be positive, reflecting (as I write) on Euro '96 – particularly the way the media set the scene for the England/Germany football match – shows just how easy it is to let the wrong emphases sow the seeds of conflict. History teachers have a very delicate line to tread with young minds!

Of course, 'what it means to be human' has no single and accepted definition; each person will answer the implicit questions according to their own philosophy of life, and the 'baggage' which that carries. The Marxist educationalist will have quite a different view of the purpose of education from one who approaches the issues from the perspective of Zen. Can there be a distinctively Christian approach? The Christian faith is, to a significant extent, a doctrinally centred religion. Throughout its history (less, but still present these days in some shape or form) has been an emphasis on right-thinking (orthodoxy) as opposed to wrong-thinking (heterodoxy). Whether one is orthodox or heterodox may often seem to depend on one's point of view; it also depends on the accidents (or providence) of history. Bearing in mind the important insight that history is written by the winners, it is sobering to reflect on where Christian orthodoxy might be today had Constantine put his weight behind Arius instead of Athanasius, or even more striking, had Charles Martel not defeated the Muslims at Poitiers in AD 732 (we certainly wouldn't be dating AD/BC, and would probably now be discussing Muslim education). The teaching of the faith in many different contexts has, over the years, been open to the charge of indoctrination – the substitution of your views for mine. Very often, not least in the schools established with the express aim of educating pupils 'in the principles of the Established Church', the charge was probably correct. That presumably was one of the reasons why the 1944 Education Act was so beset by denominational suspicions: there was then the constant fear that one denomination would be advantaged over another through its ability to run schools. The model of a school system established to promote nurture in the faith has been the predominant model of the Roman Catholic sector: 'a Catholic school, for Catholic children taught by Catholic teachers'.

However, Christian Education does need to be distinguished from Christian Nurture – enabling a child to grow in the faith. That task is much more appropriately the responsibility of the family and the faith community. But the divide can hardly be absolute, not least because the Church school is a part of that faith community (even if it is not often recognised as such), with a vocation to fulfil, somehow, in both mission and ministry. Suffice it to say the Church school will play a supportive role insofar as this does not undermine its prime responsibility for the delivery of education.

Education in a Christian context ought to reflect those values which are life-enhancing. According to the Evangelist John, Jesus came to bring abundant life. Education ought to encourage, not hinder, this process. That means that education is inevitably a risky endeavour. If we are to teach in such a way as to encourage autonomous decision-making, then we take the risk that the decisions reached might not reflect our own beliefs and values. That is why any theology of education is not far removed from a lively theology of creation. God the Creator took an enormous risk in creating free men and women; the main risk being ultimate rejection (we might even reflect that the mere placing of the Tree in the Garden of Eden was almost deliberately asking for trouble!). This is where eschatological universalists often flinch from the conclusions of their own logic, arguing that a God of love will not allow anyone to be damned eternally. The God of love (John Macquarrie, in *Principles of Christian Theology*, SCM Press, 1977, terms the Creator God as the 'One who lets be') is a God who, while never resting from his efforts to embrace all within his cosmic embrace, must presumably bow to the freedom which he himself has bestowed in grace. Someone may ultimately say 'No'. Those of us engaged in providing education in a Christian context, although not quite so eschatologically balanced ('on the edge', so to speak) must recognise the full force of what our creation-redemption-consummation theologies are saying to us. We are actually sharing in the risk of creation in and through our work with children. We may even recognise that the description 'human being' is a misnomer; we are not human beings at all, we are human in the process of becoming truly human (Macquarrie tells us that the most truly human condition is Christhood, because at that point humanity and divinity come together; those who think this is Christian Education aiming just a little too high should read the arch-orthodox Athanasius: 'He was made man, that we might be made God' *De Incarnatione* 54.3). Are we, perhaps, merely 'human becomings', on our way? And is not education all about helping us on our way?

Certainly our aim as Christian educationalists must be to enable the one who is young and dependent to grow towards independence and such autonomy that life allows (part of the creative risk means that life is precarious). In so doing we are in partnership with the parent who may or may not recognise his/her creative role; the parent who never wants to let the child grow up, or who binds the child by chains of guilt, is not a good partner in the process, and what the school is seeking to do, and the values it is seeking to commend, may even run counter to the intentions and values of parents. This makes for a real dilemma, but should not stop the Church school standing by what it believes to be right. Of course, that doesn't mean educating from a position of neutrality. There can never be (as the various curricular experiments of the 1960s and 1970s adequately demonstrated) a values vacuum. Where people pretend there is ('we are letting him decide for himself...' – often said by parents about the child's faith development), what they are really doing is allowing other, often negative, values to permeate uncontrolled. There are plenty of pernicious influences in the world just waiting to 'get in'. Advertisers, for example, are not interested in education! Here, then, is the paradox referred to above. Like the Pauline paradox 'Not I but the grace of God which was within me' (1 Corinthians 15: 10 – what D.M. Baillie called 'the paradox of grace'), the Christianised process of education will not be purely disinterested, but neither should it be indoctrinatory. But it should be distinctive, and it should be educational in enabling positive decision-making to be an inalienable human right.

But how is such distinctiveness expressed in practice in the curriculum? In *A Future in Partnership* Robert Waddington did not refer to curricular activity directly, but he did point to a variety of ways of being distinctive that ought to be reflected in the work of Church schools (p.71):

'Christian inferences are built into the ethos and teaching as signals for children to detect.'

'A place of distinctive excellence'

'a place of revelation and disclosure'

'a beacon signalling the transcendent' and so on.

Of course with the National Curriculum we no longer have the choice in making the curriculum decisions which we used to be able to make and, especially with regard to Key Stage 4, there are not many options left. Therefore curricular distinctiveness in a Church secondary school is not likely to be found in curricular additions, i.e. things done in Church schools which are not done in other schools. It will be reflected more in those curricular emphases which reflect the insights of Christian faith. Here are just a few:

- awe/fascination: in our teaching of the sciences/geography we will want children to see the natural world and the universe around us, not simply as an impersonal machine, but as an environment that ought to inspire feelings of awe and wonder in us. I am not actually suggesting that it is appropriate actively to counteract the materialist/mechanist view by explicitly parading various forms of the cosmological and teleological arguments (I'm not convinced that science lessons are the place for these regardless of whether we consider them good arguments or not!), but it is certainly appropriate to focus on the age-old human propensity to be dwarfed, surprised, etc. Theologically, such an approach fits in well with Otto's concept of God as the *'mysterium tremendum fascinans'* – that numinous presence which overwhelms, yet also fascinates and draws us. The Christian teacher will enable pupils at least to touch this mystery.

- humility: once we have experienced the wonders of our universe we begin to see (as many scientists are now saying quite openly) that we may never have all the answers; such intellectual humility is the sign of a truly educated person. In this sense 'humility' will be a cross-curricular experience, and out of it will arise a tolerance of the ideas of others. This is not to recommend a thorough-going relativism (i.e. all ideas are equally true – it just depends on your perspective), because the truly educated person will debate forcefully, albeit with love and concern for those with whom she or he is debating. We will at least understand why others see things differently from us and, with that understanding, will seek to explore truth together – wherever that exploration may lead.

- concern for truth (which, again as the Johannine Christ assures us, liberates): pathways will therefore be followed (so far as possible) without ideological bias. Of course, children will learn from their study of history and religion that what they might previously have believed to have been 'facts' are actually interpretations of human experience. They will learn that in order to interpret, we have to allow the evidence to speak to us. Sometimes the evidence may seem to undermine our dearest beliefs. Being 'led out' on the road of 'human becoming', requires us to follow where the evidence leads us, as hard as that might occasionally be.

- excellence of provision: as we have seen, Waddington dealt with this quite explicitly, and rightly so. No doubt many (or even most) schools aim for excellence, although it is quite clear that not all schools and not all teachers are achieving it. They do it because striving for excellence is a fundamental human endeavour. But it may not be a life imperative. For Christians, who see themselves made in the image and likeness of God, it is. We cannot work as Christian disciples with only limited enthusiasm, hoping that what we do will be 'all right'. To take up our crosses requires that we give all. We will never achieve perfection, but we will not be satisfied with less (Matthew 5: 48 AV – this actually refers to moral perfection, but we have already seen that it is sometimes helpful to be just a little less pedantic).

While, therefore, a Church school will seek for excellence of provision generally, it is in RE that the Church school will wish particularly to excel. This is because Church schools will recognise more than many (if not most) the importance of RE in the development of a well-educated person: the person who can make a genuinely autonomous stab at life in an ambiguous world, but who will also be open to the possibilities that lie around him or her. It is evident that in the 50+ years since the 1944 Education Act (let alone since the 'revivalist' 1988 Act), on the whole, County schools have demeaned the teaching of religious education both in terms of the derisory amount of time allowed for it in the curriculum, and the low priority given to both staffing and resourcing. But there will a genuine concern for educational, as opposed to confessional, RE, because the Church school will recognise that its responsibility for delivering the curriculum does not entail, nor does it permit, evangelism. This is often a difficult balancing act for the RE teacher in the Church school. In my school we have become used (and fairly immune) to the annual letters from some Year 9 parents who (having kept their peace about Year 8's trip to the synagogue: Jews are obviously OK for some reason – 'Ah yes; didn't Jesus have something do with Judaism'!) complain bitterly that they didn't send their children to a Church school for them to be 'taught about ethnics' and their religions! Our courteous, but tongue-biting, replies refer to things like understanding, tolerance, love, etc.; parents are often unimpressed. That is the cross the Christian RE teacher carries. It is often made heavier when some of the clergy continue to beat them with the stick: 'how come your pupils come to my confirmation class not knowing much about the Bible?' We equally courteously remind the parish clergy that they have a teaching role as well. So much for partnership!

Moral or values education, if it is given curriculum time at all, is often subsumed under (or even implicitly takes the place of) RE in many schools. Church schools will clearly recognise the importance of the link between religion and ethics, although they will neither make the mistake of thinking they are the same, nor will they fail to recognise that an ethical stance for life does not require religious commitment. It other words the Christian context will ensure that positive regard is given to the moral dimension of education. This will not simply be (although it may include) explicit teaching in RE or PSE courses; it will also permeate the whole curriculum as a dimension that affects the whole of life. The teaching of science, geography, English literature, history (to name just a few) will engage children in ethical debate appropriate to their age and experience: what are the ethical dimensions of the development of nuclear power? Do we have obligations to the Third World? What can we learn from the lives described in this piece of fiction? Has the study of the Holocaust anything to teach us? Obviously the Christian context for learning will point to ethical values which have already been carefully defined (in other words, what the Archbishop of Canterbury has described as 'privatised values', where everything is left to individual consciences, will not be proposed) within the established tradition. This of course does not solve all ethical problems, and pupils will learn that Christians continue to disagree on some central ethical issues. So once again, as our curricular emphases have made clear, this will not simply be passing on the tradition uncritically – that is not education – but it will involve taking the pupils on a journey of exploration through which they may be guided towards the establishment of their own values systems (and so contribute towards the values of society) within the Christian context that has been clearly commended by the school. We may even go further than the Archbishop of Canterbury did in a BBC interview by saying that adultery is wrong!

I have endeavoured to argue that Christian Education (the education which Church schools ought to be providing, and hence the main driving force behind the curriculum) is not a contradiction in terms; rather it is the essence of what we need to develop towards our true human nature. While Christian Education is based (as all things must be based outside the perspective of eternity) on a bedrock of ideology i.e. Christian self-understanding reflected in the historical development of creed and dogma, that bedrock cannot be all there is. It is simply (to change the metaphor) a launching-pad from which we take the leap (into the dark? Yes – but there are various lights) not only of religious faith, but of faith in humanity. The point of the launching pad is that it is an means to an end, and not an end in itself. So is Christian education.

4

Christian beliefs

A conspicuous feature of Christian belief is the juxtaposition of opposites. Christians find in the humanity and divinity of Jesus someone who was fully God and fully human: God incarnate in the person of Jesus without reducing either his divinity or his humanity. The Crucifixion and the Resurrection of Jesus reveal the pain and horror of death while asserting the glory of triumph over death. The Cross with its two aspects of the horizontal and the vertical draws symbolic attention to the truth Christians find expressed in the person of Jesus. The very centre of the Cross harmonises opposites through hope, glory and truth. Within this fundamental belief in a relationship between ourselves and God, between life and death, is the issue of how human beings treat and respond to each other.

As Christians we live and work with colleagues and families who may, or may not, share our faith. We respond to them in human terms but at the same time recognise that it is because of our faith that we hold them in such esteem. For all of us are, in our belief, created by God in his likeness and will return to him, and therefore we all share together in some form of relationship to the Creator. In crude terms we recognise all too readily our humanity with all its weaknesses. But how are we able to express to colleagues and the children in schools that we value them not just as people but as people loved of God and created by him?

Such a view has a direct link with education for it makes clear to the Church(es) and indeed to all Christians that all are not in education for what they can get out of it but for what they can contribute. If one of the fundamental dimensions of an educational commitment is the recognition that Christ is at the very centre of relationships, with our peers and our pupils, then the values about which we as members of society are deeply concerned become central. Learning will not be an end in itself but shot through with the values and meaning of human relationships.

These views will have a direct effect on the choice of values Christians wish to promote, safeguard and inculcate in schools as a whole, as well as in the defined curriculum. Lip-service to them is not sufficient. Acknowledging God as Creator ensures that Christians are fully committed to their colleagues as well as their pupils and indeed to the whole world. For many, this will be demonstrated through the views they express in the classroom as well as in their contribution to the ethos of the school; for others, their faith will not be expressed overtly but will form the core of inner strength and purpose. Caught up within this complex response to God is integrity, for with such integrity, commitment to one's faith must be expressed in every situation. The power of integrity as an aspect of faith cannot be over-estimated; it is a quality recognised and respected by all even when the beliefs themselves are not shared.

For every Christian healing and wholeness, service and worship are linked together, for every person is unique, created by God with unlimited potential for growth.

5

The values in education and the community

At the time of writing the Schools Curriculum and Assessment Authority (SCAA) is on the verge of producing a statement on the values society has in common. The principal task is how we, as post-modern society, can build on agreed core values without creating dissension.

Society

We value truth, justice, human rights, the rule of law and collective effort for the common good. In particular we value families as sources of love and support for all their members and of the basis of a society in which people care for others.

On the basis of these values, we should:

- understand and carry out our responsibilities as citizens;
- refuse to support values or actions that may be harmful to individuals or communities;
- support families in raising children and caring for dependants;
- support the institution of marriage;
- recognise that the love and commitment required for a secure and happy childhood can be found in families of different kinds;
- help people to know about the law and legal processes;
- respect the law and encourage others to do so;
- respect religious and cultural differences;

- promote opportunities for all;
- support those who cannot, by themselves, sustain a dignified lifestyle;
- promote participation in the democratic process;
- contribute to, as well as benefit fairly from, economic and cultural resources;
- make truth, goodwill and integrity priorities in public and private life.

Relationships

We value others for themselves, not only for what they have or what they can do for us. We value relationships as fundamental to the development and fulfilment of ourselves and others and to the good of the community.

On the basis of these values, we should:

- respect others;
- care for others and exercise goodwill in our dealings with them;
- show others they are valued;
- work co-operatively with others;
- earn loyalty, trust and confidence;
- respect the privacy and property of others;
- resolve disputes peacefully.

The self

We value ourselves as unique human beings capable of spiritual, moral, intellectual and physical growth and development.

On the basis of these values, we should:

- try to understand our own character, our strengths and weaknesses;
- develop a sense of self-esteem;
- try to discover meaning and purpose in our lives and decide, on the basis of this, how we believe that our lives should be lived;
- make responsible use of our talents, rights and opportunities;
- strive, throughout life, for knowledge, wisdom and understanding;
- take responsibility, within our capabilities, for our own lives.

The environment

We value both the natural world and manmade environment as the basis of life and a source of wonder and inspiration.

On the basis of these values we should:

- understand the place of human beings within nature;
- understand our duties to other species;
- ensure that development can be justified in the light of our responsibility to maintain a sustainable environment for future generations;
- preserve balance and diversity in nature wherever possible;
- preserve areas of beauty and interest for future generations;
- repair, wherever possible, habitats damaged by human development.

If SCAA is to produce examples of good practice and curriculum guidance for schools based on these broadly agreed core values, then Church schools will need to ensure that their own religious ethos underpins all their work. SCAA is a secular body; it will not produce guidelines for Church schools, although it could well use different models used by Church schools as exemplar material. Christians should not lose the opportunity to contribute vigorously to the debate about values, for the consequences of the current debate will spill, are spilling, over into the whole curriculum. The 'subject isolationism' mentioned by Ruth Deakin Crick will find it difficult to resist a 'values' audit. For Church schools that audit should have taken place and be firmly *in situ*. If the Government is to insist on the importance of values and value clarification in all schools, then Church schools will need to be able to point to the place of Christian values in the curriculum and in the whole life of the school.

For it is in the life of a Church school that the Christian religion, in its various shades and interpretations, should be seen as a faith by which to live. The 'values' of the SCAA document, in whatever form they are finally agreed and published, will be contextualised, or should be, in the commonality and theology of the school. Each Church school will explore the meaning of its Church foundation differently, bearing in mind its governors, staff, parents and pupils, but much of the educational work – praise and punishment, pastoral care, forgiveness, celebration, grief, careful pedagogy, etc. – will be true for *all* schools. The Church school has to root all of these in the earth of a living vital religious faith.

This is why the SCAA exercise is valuable. It seeks to discover agreement and consensus over a central core. Then it will be up to the schools, and Christians in those schools, to give that core life and vitality: a context which has a relevance for the pupils and the communities from which they come.

One of the disappointments over the last few years since the debate on Spiritual and Moral Development gained a higher profile is the way in which Government agencies like OFSTED and SCAA have, in public documents, given less priority than they might to the very distinctive contribution made by the 32 per cent of schools that are Church schools (January 1995). If such schools really are part of a dual system and have so many pupils (12.25 per cent attend Church schools (17.5 per cent of primary pupils)), why are Government educational agencies so loath to acknowledge them in their publications? The OFSTED *Handbook for Inspection* struggles to find appropriate criteria for the inspection of spiritual development and perhaps pays insufficient attention to the contribution the ethos of a school can make to the spiritual development of the pupil. The earlier SCAA publication *Spiritual and Moral Development – a discussion paper* (1995) (an earlier NCC document published unamended) identified a number of key issues central for spiritual development. None of these key issues made any reference to a sense of community or the way in which spiritual development can develop in, or be fostered by, a living vibrant community. Surely the development of a vibrant school community has implications for all schools, and especially Church schools?

6

Spiritual development: An approach for all schools

Robin Protheroe

hat on earth is 'spiritual development', for heaven's sake? Difficult to define, for a start. It applies to something distinctly human, not necessarily experienced through the physical senses or capable of being expressed through everyday language. It has to do with our search for our real selves; our responses to questions raised by death, suffering and beauty; our engagement with good and evil; the search for meaning in life and values by which to live; relationships with others and, for believers, with God.

Seen in this way, spiritual development is for everyone. From childhood on, we are all, believers and not, in a process of being moved by beauty or kindness, hurt by the selfishness of others; growing in awareness of when and how to control our emotions; learning to express our imagination and insight creatively in various ways; becoming aware of our individuality and developing self-respect; being inspired and awestruck by experiences which strike us as mysterious or awesome.

How do we as teachers support and nurture this process of spiritual development? One possible approach is direct, personal and intimate. It may involve introducing pupils to the appreciation of their own inner life by teaching them ways of quiet and still reflectiveness, self-awareness and self-observation. It may provide them with structured experiences of ways of relating to one another, and invite them to consider how they feel as they respond. This approach is outlined by writers like Michael Beesley, Mary Stone, David Hay et al. It has deep roots in the Christian tradition. Many teachers who have tried it report that children enjoy being helped to explore the experience of silence, and their own thoughts and feelings. Other teachers and parents are concerned about what they perceive as influences from eastern religions.

A complementary, indirect and non-controversial approach involves looking at the whole life of the school from the perspective of spiritual development. Does each 'subject area' ask pupils to consider specific questions about values? Are pupils encouraged to question the possible shortcomings of the ways they receive impressions, through vision, logic and language? Are pupils helped to think about ways in which good and bad habits are formed? Are they led to question assumptions about what a 'person' is, and what gives a person value? Are pupils encouraged and supported when they question traditional ways of doing things, and want to explore new ways?

Looking specifically at the scientific areas of the curriculum, are pupils required to notice that, while science provides many significant answers to the question 'how?', it is important to go on to ask 'why?' Do pupils question the extent to which they are their bodies? Is the development of technology set in the context of human values? Despite the practical impossibility of setting up 'disclosure experiences' of awe, it is worth asking; is wonder encouraged? To be faced unexpectedly even with a visual cliché like a dew-spangled spider's web can trigger insight.

In the areas of language and the arts, are pupils made aware of the limitations of all forms of expression? That there are some human experiences which can leave one 'lost for words'? Christians say that God is ineffable, beyond description, great. But then we 'eff' him all the time, and are tempted to feel that we have got him taped. Are pupils encouraged to see the power of words and their influence on experience? That experience is divided up in different ways in different languages? Do teachers avoid giving 'right' answers to questions like 'What is the meaning of this poem/symbol'? Are pupils encouraged to take a lively interest in what goes on in their own imaginations? Are they given a sense of their own 'inner world'? Are they given opportunities to imagine themselves in another person's shoes?

In religious education and collective worship, is it made clear that religious activities are part of a search for meaning which goes beyond the activities themselves? That they are an expression of believers' concern with ultimate reality? Are pupils given the opportunity to explore the depth of symbolism, not learning to 'translate' or 'decode' they symbols they study, but seeing them as expressing something beyond ordinary expression? Are pupils' (or anyone else's) descriptions of experiences of the numinous or mysterious or awe-ful treated with respect and appropriately valued?

When we look at our school life from this perspective, of 'the beyond in the midst', many of us will be surprised and relieved to find that we have been engaged in the spiritual development of our pupils all the time without being fully aware of it. Heightened awareness and sensitivity will enable us to build on foundations we have already laid. And we shall have the reward of discovering yet again that the young people who are often perceived as being objects of our teaching can, from their own inner depths, actually teach us a great deal.

Bibliography

M. Beesley, *Stilling*, Salisbury, Diocesan Board of Education, 1990

M.K. Stone, *Don't Just Do Something, Sit There*, RMEP, 1995

D. Hay et al, *New Methods in RE*, Oliver and Boyd, 1990

Conclusion

Why education?

One of the most important requirements of being a Christian is to study the Bible and to engage with the text in the light of personal experience and the teaching of the Church. The history of the Church has occasionally been a struggle with education, yet whenever the Church has rejected the advances of science and education it has been less than true to the challenge of Jesus. It has sought on occasion to hide behind the closed face of bigotry rather than respond to the new issues and the questions posed by the advances in science as the way of discovering the hand of God at work. The advance of education and the growing body of knowledge of our world place a responsibility upon all Christians to seek to understand and to interpret the whole revelation of God in Christ.

Christians are on a pilgrimage. They are followers of the way and look forward in hope. Life on earth cannot be perfect; Christians have to live in the world and struggle with its imperfections. Christians will hold the vision of Christ before them as they seek to recognise the presence of God in human institutions. This is one of the challenges that they face. How is hope for the future lived out in the reality of the present? The Christian religion continuously relives its history through its festivals, its teaching, and in the celebration of the Eucharist, for the past is eternally present; time is transcended as Christians respond to present needs with both the past and future in their minds. By interpreting the teaching of Jesus and applying it to the challenges of the next century, a Christian response to the current situation may be found. It may lead to controversy and dissension, but the search for Truth – in personal devotion and commitment, in the Gospels and in the Church – is crucial to all who confess their allegiance to Christ. Such allegiance transcends the quotations of a selected number of scriptural texts. In his teachings Jesus asked questions; he probed, he required insight, he asked for understanding, he challenged his hearers to

Conclusion

respond. Yet even he appeared to have times when he had to search for the true meaning of his mission. His life was the epitome of an educational self-understanding and the search for Truth. He shared his insight and interpretation in an open, non-condemnatory way as the exemplary leader.

Contributors

Roy Hughes, who reflects on the very specific links between Religious Education and History in the context of Humanities, is the Head of St Paul's Church of England Primary School (New Windsor), Salford. Few of the pupils have direct links with the church outside the school context and the school has to find ways of introducing religious and Christian values into the whole curriculum.

This theme is developed by **Tricia Kirkham**, Headteacher of Holy Trinity Church of England Voluntary Aided Primary School, Yeovil. She explores ways in which a Church school can affirm its Christian foundation while continuing to meet the needs of the National Curriculum.

Ruth Deakin Crick was the Headteacher of Oak Hill School, Bristol, with a vision to ensure that the Christian dimension of every aspect of the curriculum would be available to pupils.

These three contributions build upon each other for they begin with the specific but broaden into a whole school concern.

Peter Shepherd is an Anglican clergyman and Head of Canon Slade Church of England Grant Maintained Secondary School, Bolton. While addressing the same concerns as the three previous contributors, he adopts a more theological approach and applies a series of theological criteria to the management of the curriculum. He is a member of the Schools' Committee of the Board of Education of the General Synod.

Robin Protheroe is also an Anglican clergyman and is the Diocesan Director of Education in the Diocese of Bristol. He believes that teaching pupils 'ways of quiet and still reflectiveness' has deep roots in the Christian tradition.

Alan Brown, Director of the National Society's London RE Centre and a Deputy Secretary of the Society, is also Schools Officer (RE) of the General Synod Board of Education. He is the author of several publications, including *The Multi-Faith Church School* and *Primary School Worship*.

THE NATIONAL SOCIETY

T he National Society (Church of England) for Promoting Religious Education supports everyone involved in Christian education – teachers, school governors, students, parents, clergy, parish and diocesan education teams – with the resources of its RE centres, courses, conferences and archives.

Founded in 1811, the Society was chiefly responsible for setting up the nationwide network of Church schools in England and Wales, and still helps them with legal and administrative advice for headteachers and governors. It was also a pioneer in teacher education through the Church colleges. The Society now provides resources for those responsible for RE and worship in any school, lecturers and students in colleges, and clergy and lay people in parish education. It publishes a wide range of books and booklets and two magazines, *Crosscurrent* (free to members) and *Together with Children*.

The National Society is a voluntary body which works in partnership with the Church of England General Synod Board of Education and the Division for Education of the Church of Wales. An Anglican society, it also operates ecumenically, and helps to promote inter-faith education and dialogue through its RE centres.

For a free resources catalogue and details of individual, corporate and associate membership contact:

> The General Secretary
> The National Society
> Church House
> Great Smith Street
> London SW1P 3NZ
> Telephone: 0171-222 1672
> Fax: 0171-233 2592